HE IS COMING

An Advent Devotional · Based on the Gospels

HE IS HERE

by NANA VINAR

To my spiritual family: Grace Church of Chapel Hill. You are the soil that has grown my heart and my family. It's been my privilege to serve you for over twenty years. My prayer is for you to experience Jesus deeply. He is coming. He is here.

CONTENTS

This devotional will transform your experience of the Christmas season! You'll think about and talk to God, hearing words of hope for your heart. I recommend finding a quiet place, perhaps with a cup of tea or coffee. Open to the day's devotional and begin to read slowly, taking into your heart the meaning of God's words. As you read the prayer, pray the words to your Heavenly Father in a personal way. Spend an extra moment to listen to and hear what God has to say back to you. For the daily finale, read the declaration aloud with faith that God is at work. He is listening, and He is eager to move mountains on your behalf. As you believe in your heart and confess with your tongue, you will speak faith-filled words; your heart will engage and join with a "Yes!" to each word. You are preparing for His coming in an eternal way. He is coming! He is here!

BASED ON THE GOSPELS

Jesus is coming. Advent is anticipation, the building of expectation as we look forward to His birth. From now until Christmas, let the reality of His coming affect your daily lives. Let it build anticipation for celebrating His arrival on Christmas Day.

Jesus is here. We are acknowledging how He is also here at this moment to work in our hearts. Perhaps our annual celebration of Jesus' coming to Earth is practice for anticipating His second coming when He will renew all things.

This Advent Season, begin to soak in the words of Luke, Matthew, and John and apply them to your daily life. He is coming. He is here.

God highly values the time of preparation

"'And he will go before him in the spirit and power of Elijah, to turn the hearts of the fathers to the children, and the disobedient to the wisdom of the just, to make ready for the Lord a people prepared.'"

Preparation is spiritual work. God strategically sent John the Baptist ahead of Jesus to begin the plowing of our hearts, so we would be ready to hear and receive all that Jesus said. The Holy Spirit led John to seed inner transformation in the hearts of the hearers.

Could your preparation time during this Advent Season be growing a readiness to say "yes" to Jesus? How can you seek a soft, willing, open, obedient heart?

PRAYER: *"Lord, give me eyes to see what I don't see. Loosen my grip on my normal way of thinking, so I can reach with openness for new lessons You have for me. I want to be ready to receive Your work in my life."*

DECLARATION: *"He is coming. I will focus on Jesus' coming during this season of Advent and let my anticipation grow. Jesus is coming to turn my heart from my way to His way. Yes, He is coming, but He is also here right now—today. He is softening my heart; He is near."*

Our hearts yearn for His nearness

"And he came to her and said, 'Greetings, O favored one, the Lord is with you!'"

The angel's message to Mary encapsulates all that our hearts want from God: His acceptance and His presence. These words to Mary sustained her through ridicule, doubt, discomfort, loneliness, and pain. Her connection to God the Father, her awareness of His accessibility, and her dependence on His approval carried her through her unique situation.

Can you hear God whispering to you a message like the angel's to Mary? "Greetings, O favored one, the Lord is with you!" What false thinking do you need to fight to hear Him speak His favor to you today?

PRAYER: *"Jesus, will you help me feel Your smile on my life today? Help me live with the moment-by-moment awareness that You are right beside me."*

DECLARATION: *"He is coming. Jesus is coming to adjust my thinking. I am His favorite child, and He is with me. As I agree with Him, I feel more and more free. Not only is He coming, He is here with me today, ready to walk me through all I am facing. His heart is for me."*

God never tires of saying, "Do not fear"

"An angel of the Lord appeared to him in a dream, saying, 'Joseph, son of David, do not fear to take Mary as your wife, for that which is conceived in her is from the Holy Spirit.'"

Joseph found himself in the center of a miracle where he felt vulnerable, uncertain, and embarrassed, but God's stabilizing command not to fear helped Joseph glimpse part of the bigger picture. The Holy Spirit was at work in this miracle to change the course of history for our redemption. Joseph's trust in God's voice led him to freeing obedience.

When concerns arise in your heart about an uncertain turn of events, how can you lean on God for courage to trust in His plan? What miracle may God be orchestrating behind the scenes?

PRAYER: *"Lord, when big or little fears pursue me, help me to see where Your Holy Spirit is moving. I want to trust Your big plan, even when the part I see is woefully uncertain. Help me view fear as a reminder to talk to You."*

DECLARATION: *"He is coming. My God is working His grand plan for the world, for the church, and for me. I can trust His goodness to work miracles out of uncertainties. Yes, He is coming, but He is also here right now, multiplying my trust in Him. He is my Fear-taker."*

God sent His Son with an intentional purpose: to save us from our sins

"She will bear a son, and you shall call his name Jesus, for he will save his people from their sins."

God called His Son "Jesus," which means "the Lord is salvation." Every time the people spoke His name, they were affirming His divine mission to save. He came to forgive us—to set us on a new path of freedom.

If you have bowed your knee to Jesus and invited Him to sit on the throne of your life, you have been rescued into His family! Have you asked Jesus to preside over all the parts of your life? Receive the forgiveness of your sins from Jesus today.

PRAYER: *"Lord, I belong to You; I'm grateful to be Your son or daughter. I speak Your name in awe that You would come for me and grant me the miracle of forgiveness. And I speak Your name for those who do not believe in You yet."*

DECLARATION: *"He is coming. Jesus is coming to save those who sin, including me. In every part of my life, I bow my knee to Jesus, my Lord. Yes, He is coming, but He is also here right now, offering me grace to walk this life with Him—100% forgiven. I am free. He is my powerful Savior."*

Ask God your questions from a basis of faith

"And Mary said to the angel, 'How will this be, since I am a virgin?'"

Mary must have had a multitude of feelings and opinions and curiosities arise as God handed her the role of mother of Jesus. Yet, she courageously asks only this one question, which attests to the depth of her relationship with God. Behind her question is a settledness that God is all-good, all-loving, and all-wise.

What questions do you have for God? Are you convinced of His completely good and unchanging character? Do you believe He causes all things in your life to work for good?

PRAYER: *"Lord, when questions bubble up inside my mind, help me bring them to You, knowing Your character is not under scrutiny. Help me to bring You all my thoughts and concerns, because I know You want to carry them for me."*

DECLARATION: *"He is coming. I believe Jesus is coming to converse with me every day. He listens, takes note, and answers me, filling my heart with peace and guidance. Not only is He coming, but He is also here with me today, showing me His reliable goodness. He is my Friend."*

Surrender is freedom

"And Mary said, 'Behold, I am the servant of the Lord; let it be to me according to your word.'"

In the face of shocking news, Mary reveals a decision she had probably made long before this moment: she lives to serve God. Her life purpose is to glorify her God. She doesn't complain that her life course just got redirected; she surrenders to God's greater plan.

How many things have you held onto tightly only to discover they were holding you back from God's greater plan in your life? Have you heard it said, "Take care of yourself, because no one else will"? What would it look like if you trusted God to care more for you than you can?

PRAYER: *"Lord, I acknowledge that Your way is higher than mine and Your plan for me is greater than mine. Because I trust in You, I surrender to Your care my control over this day and my future days."*

DECLARATION: *"He is coming. He is coming to free me from my own ideas. He is beckoning me to trust Him even more. Yes, He is coming, but He is also here right now, bringing an assurance that He is worthy to be trusted completely. His plans for me are good."*

Our faith allows blessings to come

"And blessed is she who believed that there would be a fulfillment of what was spoken to her from the Lord."

When Elizabeth heard Mary's voice of greeting, Elizabeth experienced the internal joyous jump of her baby, John, and the Holy Spirit revealed to her that Mary was carrying their Savior. Elizabeth's husband, Zechariah, had struggled to believe his barren wife would conceive; consequently, he spent at least nine months unable to speak. In contrast, Elizabeth, Zechariah's wife, was witnessing Mary's inspiring faith in God's Word. Through Mary's faith, blessings come to Elizabeth and many thereafter.

What promise from God's Word are you believing? Can you think of a time when God spoke to you and then fulfilled what was spoken? How does that remembrance build your faith to trust Him now?

PRAYER: *"Lord, I want to be one who is quick to believe what You say. I bring You the doubts that cross my mind, and I leave them with You. Please take my faith and grow it."*

DECLARATION: *"He is coming. Jesus is coming with blessings to pour out on all those who believe, including me. I believe every word that God speaks! Yes, He is coming, but He is also here today, increasing my ability to take Him at His word. He is a Miracle-Worker."*

A true view of God brings forth heartfelt praise

"My soul magnifies the Lord, and my spirit rejoices in God my Savior, for he has looked on the humble estate of his servant. For behold, from now on all generations will call me blessed; for he who is mighty has done great things for me, and holy is his name."

Mary overflows with joy in this song of praise to her God. She speaks of her servant identity; she is elated by the opportunity to serve her God in this way. She sees her Lord as mighty, holy, generous, and compassionate. He is quick to bestow blessings on her, so her heart overflows with praise.

How might your view of God differ from Mary's? What great things has God done for you that inspire your praise?

PRAYER: *"Lord, lead me into this kind of joyous connection with You that I would delight to serve You and praise You because of who You are. Show me where I see You inaccurately; I want nothing to stand between us."*

DECLARATION: *"He is coming. Jesus is coming to bring uncontainable joy to my heart. His hands are full of generosity for me. Yes, He is coming, but He is also here right now, tenderly leading me into a humble servant identity. He is my gracious Lord."*

God is moved by our hunger and need for Him

"He has filled the hungry with good things, and the rich he has sent away empty."

In Mary's song of praise, she enumerates the great things God has done, and then she says something curious: He sends the rich away empty. Why wouldn't He equally fill the hungry and the rich? The hungry are the humble who acknowledge their need and ask God to fill it. The rich are the proud who think they have all they need. Sometimes we have not because we ask not (James 4:2).

In what areas of your life do you bring your requests to God with humility? In what areas of your life do you tend to rely on your own strength, not asking God for help?

PRAYER: *"Lord, I want to be more honest with You than I have been before. I truly need You in every way. Help me be humble and hungry when I come to You, because then You respond by providing all I need."*

DECLARATION: *"He is coming. He is coming to show me how empty I am and then fill me with all I need. Yes, He is coming, but He is also here right now, helping me embrace the grace I need every day. I don't have to pretend to be capable on my own; He is my Provider."*

Spreading our good news to others
points to God's greatness

"And her neighbors and relatives heard that the Lord had shown great mercy to her, and they rejoiced with her."

When she gave birth to John, Elizabeth spread her exciting news to all around her, and they shared her joy. The rejoicing was contagious! They all knew she had been unable to conceive for years, so this miracle child pointed to God's merciful blessing. John's birth confirmed to all the hearers that God is powerful and He keeps His promises.

How has God been merciful and good to you recently? With whom could you share your good news?

PRAYER: *"Lord, when I consider how You have moved powerfully in my life, my heart swells in gratitude to You. Guide me to tell those around me the story of how great You are to me."*

DECLARATION: *"He is coming. Jesus is coming with power and mercy toward those who would believe in Him. He is opening people's eyes to see the magnitude of His greatness. Yes, He is coming, but He is also here right now, highlighting the redemptive work He has done in my heart. I am filled with joy. He is my Joy-bringer."*

God works openly, so His fame
will spread far and wide

"And immediately his mouth was opened and his tongue loosed, and he spoke, blessing God. And fear came on all their neighbors. And all these things were talked about through all the hill country of Judea."

When her baby was born, Elizabeth called him John, which sparked curiosity because everyone assumed he would be named for his father, Zechariah. Then, as Zechariah confirmed the name John, God opened Zechariah's mouth, breaking his nine-month stint of silence. Zechariah blessed God for the demonstration of His power—which all the people witnessed.

How do you see God's power working in your life? How can you trust His power and His presence more deeply?

PRAYER: *"Lord, I want to see Your power moving in my life and in my community. Help me to see more of what You are doing because I know You are always at work. As I look to You, grow my faith to sense Your presence all around me today."*

DECLARATION: *"He is coming. My Jesus is coming to show Himself to those who do not yet believe. He is revealing truth, working miracles, and changing lives. Yes, He is coming, but He is also here right now, working in my difficulties and drawing me closer to Him. I feel His love as He tends to my heart."*

Jesus is our salvation

"Blessed be the Lord God of Israel, for he has visited and redeemed his people and has raised up a horn of salvation for us in the house of his servant David."

When his mouth is opened, Zechariah erupts into an inspired prophecy about Jesus' works to come. The Holy Spirit has revealed to Zechariah that Jesus is the fulfillment of the old prophecies of salvation and redemption.

Consider how far God has brought you from where you began in your walk with Him. How has God redeemed your life? For what purpose?

PRAYER: *"Lord, thank You for coming to Earth in the form of a man to save me from my original independent path of sin. I am so grateful Jesus has saved me, so I can have a peaceful and close relationship with God."*

DECLARATION: *"He is coming. Jesus is coming to redeem me from my life of selfish ambition and self-absorption. The God of the whole earth is coming for me. Yes, He is coming, but He is also here right now, pleased with His choosing of me. He is my Savior, not just once but every day."*

God sent His Son to guide us into peace with Him

"And you, child, will be called the prophet of the Most High; for you will go before the Lord to prepare his ways, to give knowledge of salvation to his people in the forgiveness of their sins, because of the tender mercy of our God, whereby the sunrise shall visit us from on high to give light to those who sit in darkness and in the shadow of death, to guide our feet into the way of peace."

Filled with the Holy Spirit, Zechariah prophesies about his son John who will go before Jesus to prepare the people's hearts to receive their Savior. Even before Jesus' birth, Zechariah tells those who are listening that Jesus is the Light who is coming to dispel their darkness and save them from death. I imagine Zechariah taught John all that the Holy Spirit poured into him that day.

When you consider approaching God to talk to Him, do you feel as though something stands between the two of you? In what way has Jesus helped you feel forgiven? How could you take a step "into the way of peace" with God today?

PRAYER: *"Lord, I'm aware that my sin creates distance between You and me. Thank You for taking the guilt and shame from my sin and offering me forgiveness. I'm so grateful that I can run right up to You with arms outstretched because I have ongoing peace with my Heavenly Father."*

DECLARATION: *"He is coming. Jesus is coming to forgive, to have mercy, and to shine light on the dark places in my heart. Yes, He is coming, but He is also here right now, saying that I can approach Him freely with guilt-free peace in my heart. He is my Prince of Peace."*

The God who knows the end from the beginning is with us

"All this took place to fulfill what the Lord had spoken by the prophet: 'Behold, the virgin shall conceive and bear a son, and they shall call his name Immanuel' (which means, God with us)."

Hundreds and hundreds of years before Mary gave birth to Jesus, the prophets foretold the Savior's arrival from a virgin. Why did God begin to tell His people in advance—so long before Jesus came? He was demonstrating His authority over all time and space, so that He would be glorified. When Jesus came, He did just that: He pointed to His Father.

What does the phrase "God with us" mean to you today?

PRAYER: *"Holy Creator of the Universe, thank You for sending Jesus to Earth, so I could experience closeness with You without any guilt and shame standing between You and me. Help me walk every day with a greater awareness of Your nearness."*

DECLARATION: *"He is coming. Jesus is coming to span the chasm between His holiness and my humanity, for me and for those who don't know Him yet. Yes, He is coming, but He is also here right now, bringing His presence into the hidden and closed-off portions of my heart. He is with all of me."*

This surprising miracle will bring joy to every heart

"And the angel said to them, 'Fear not, for behold, I bring you good news of great joy that will be for all the people.'"

Perhaps the shepherds had established a reputation for spreading news across an area while they guided their flocks from pasture to pasture. Acknowledging the shocking method of his announcement, the angel told the shepherds not to be afraid. He certainly had their rapt attention as he delivered the "good news of great joy."

How has the good news of the gospel impacted your life? When you're facing something overwhelming, how does this good news steady your heart? Who do you know who would want to hear this good news as you have experienced it?

PRAYER: *"Lord, Your coming for me is indeed the greatest of happenings in my life. As You have touched my life and set me free, please show me who else is ready to hear about Your coming for them."*

DECLARATION: *"He is coming. Jesus is coming with joy for all who hear Him. His message changes our gloom and despair into rejoicing. Yes, He is coming, but He is also here right now, enabling me to rejoice by lifting my eyes from today's issues and fixing them on my Savior."*

Our purpose is to praise God like the angels did after the announcement to the unsuspecting shepherds

"And suddenly there was with the angel a multitude of the heavenly host praising God and saying, 'Glory to God in the highest, and on earth peace among those with whom he is pleased!'"

Bringing glory to God is the purpose of our existence here on Earth, and at the incarnation, the angelic choir came to demonstrate how to do so. Following the angels' example, we can say, "Look at what the Almighty has done!"

In what ways can your life bring attention and honor to God? When your gaze is on the things God has accomplished, in what way do you feel His peace rising in your heart?

PRAYER: *"Lord, I want my whole life to say, 'Look at what the Almighty has done!' Help me see what You're doing and focus on it, because You are worthy of my praise."*

DECLARATION: *"He is coming. Jesus is coming to bring peace to my heart because He is pleased with me. Yes, He is coming, but He is also here right now, leading me to a calm space of trust where I can stop trying to earn His approval. My Jesus loves me."*

Mary demonstrates to us how to manage her thoughts with faith

"But Mary treasured up all these things, pondering them in her heart."

We can imagine all that Mary could have done instead of treasuring the words of God that came through the angel and the shepherds. However, she wisely took hold of God's words and let them grow in her heart. Treasuring and pondering the promises of God can lead to a peaceful, stabilized heart.

What words from God do you treasure in your heart? You could hold offenses near and replay them often to feel that rush of indignation. You could give space to fearful thoughts that claim they need frequent attention. Instead of those options, what promises from God do you want to spend time pondering?

PRAYER: *"Lord, I want to hear Your words to me and hold them close in my heart. Help me filter what I allow my mind and heart to ponder."*

DECLARATION: *"He is coming. Jesus is coming to fill my mind and heart with His words of truth and life. His words are growing inside me. Yes, He is coming, but He is also here right now, leading me to store up the priceless promises that He speaks to me."*

God sent Jesus to show us the way to the Father

"For my eyes have seen your salvation that you have prepared in the presence of all peoples, a light for revelation to the Gentiles, and for glory to your people Israel."

Simeon saw baby Jesus in the temple and knew by the Spirit that He was the salvation of the world. God planted pieces of revelation in various people along the way to point to the coming of the Savior. Mankind was in darkness and needed the thick, heavy cloud lifted to see and understand and receive Jesus as Savior.

When you were groping in darkness, fumbling and trying to make sense of life, what sparked the opening of your eyes to see Jesus? Was it a friend who offered you their experience of freely relating to God? Was it God speaking to you through the Bible? In what area of life would you like God to light your path?

PRAYER: *"Lord, at times I am still in some darkness. Please open my eyes to see more of You. Send Your light to reveal Yourself to me, so I can walk more closely with You."*

DECLARATION: *"He is coming. Jesus is coming to pave the way between my wayward heart and the Father. Yes, He is coming, but He is also here right now, shining His gracious light deep into my heart and removing sneaky lies to plant His grace and truth today. Jesus is my Revealer."*

God works in our hearts to inspire us to seek Him

"Where is he who has been born king of the Jews? For we saw his star when it rose and have come to worship him."

The so-called "wise men" were indeed wise as they searched for the coming Messiah, noticed His star, and began an investigatory trek in order to worship Him! Their hearts were open to God. They were drawn by Him, and they responded to Him.

When you feel an inner nudge you think is from God, what do you do? To what extent do you feel ready to obey when you hear His voice?

PRAYER: *"Lord, I want to increase my sensitivity to hear Your voice speaking to my heart. Draw my heart to hear You and obey You every day. I surrender to You. Your voice brings such comfort to me."*

DECLARATION: *"He is coming. God is sending His Son to speak clearly to me, so I can worship Him. As I respond to Him, He is making me wiser. Yes, He is coming, but He is also here right now, softening the harder parts of my heart to receive Him. His voice is the tender and guiding voice that I long to hear."*

Jesus is worthy of our honor, our worship, and our gifts

"And going into the house, they saw the child with Mary his mother, and they fell down and worshiped him. Then, opening their treasures, they offered him gifts, gold and frankincense and myrrh."

What reverence and honor these wise men demonstrated as they traveled to worship Jesus as a child! Jesus received these expensive gifts befitting a king. Surely the wise men's hearts belonged to their King Jesus.

Jesus has zero needs, because He is God, but He delights in our affection and attention and gifts. If you could give Him what you value most, what would it be? Is He worthy of your time? Is He worthy of your life?

PRAYER: *"Lord, I belong to You. I want to hold nothing back from my Jesus. Show me the parts of my life I have reserved for myself; I want to give You those parts as well. All the things I give to You are in the very best hands. I trust You with all that I am."*

DECLARATION: *"He is coming. Jesus is coming to change my thinking. He is showing me that I owe Him all. I would be nothing without His presence in my life. Yes, He is coming, but He is also here right now, beckoning me closer and deeper into trusting who He is. He is my King."*

Man's devious plans cannot
thwart God's ultimate plan

"Then Herod, when he saw that he had been tricked by the wise men, became furious, and he sent and killed all the male children in Bethlehem and in all that region who were two years old or under, according to the time that he had ascertained from the wise men."

As horrific as Herod's actions are to consider, we can see that his evil intentions did not accomplish his purpose: killing Jesus. Evil happens in this world for now because of sin, but God's plan to sacrifice His Son Jesus on our behalf to rescue us from our own ways is not interrupted. God's plan—involving you and me—is already established and cannot be wrecked.

So many parts of our lives cannot be understood, particularly the "why" of certain events. Is your heart reassured that God's plan involves you and that you cannot mess it up? In what situation of your life do you need to trust that God's purpose will not be thwarted?

PRAYER: *"Father, I am so grateful that You see the end from the beginning and that Your plan for me is good. Thank You for crafting a plan of redemption for me, so that I can have a close relationship with You."*

DECLARATION: *"He is coming. My Jesus is coming to wield His power over all the evil in the world and in my heart. His strength brings me security. Yes, He is coming, but He is also here right now, holding me when evil seems impending. He is my Strong Redeemer."*

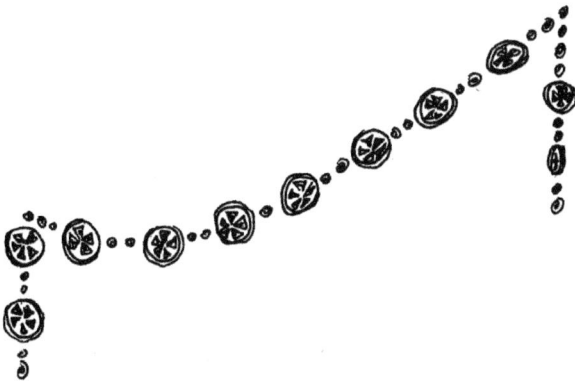

God has always existed, and He's the originator of all good things

"In the beginning was the Word, and the Word was with God, and the Word was God. He was in the beginning with God. All things were made through him, and without him was not anything made that was made. In him was life, and the life was the light of men. The light shines in the darkness, and the darkness has not overcome it."

One of the primary deceptions humanity faces is that true life can be found outside of God Himself. Adam and Eve looked beyond what God had given to them, believing the forbidden fruit promised a more appealing life than they had at the moment. God's life and light are what our hearts are actually wanting when we make decisions every day, but sometimes sin's false promises fool us.

If God has always existed, and He's the originator of all good things, to what extent would you agree that His life is what you're desiring? When acknowledging that you have made a sinful choice, can you recognize the empty promise hidden within your choice?

PRAYER: *"Lord, thank You for coming with the authentic life that I need. Help me see through the lies that sin whispers to me: that I can find life or joy or fulfillment on my own path. I am so grateful You shine Your light into the darkness!"*

DECLARATION: *"He is coming. Jesus is coming to put an end to deception and sin. Yes, He is coming, but He is also here right now, guiding me into His path of true life. He is opening my eyes to free me from going my own way. Jesus is my Light."*

God helps us believe in Him and join His family

"He came to his own, and his own people did not receive him. But to all who did receive him, who believed in his name, he gave the right to become children of God."

God is the Supreme Giver. He gives us the ability to hear His good news, He softens our hearts to say "yes" to Him, and He brings us close to Him as His dear children. As beloved members of His family, we have unhindered access to God—no matter what. In addition, our God continues to help us lean on Him for all that we need and choose His ways over our own.

Have you opened your heart to believe in God and join His family? He is eagerly waiting to forgive you and welcome you into His family. You can receive Him today. As a child of God, to what extent do you believe you can approach God and be fully accepted by Him?

PRAYER: *"Lord, thank You for drawing me close. I lay down all my defenses and excuses about my sin in exchange for Your righteousness. I love being Your child."*

DECLARATION: *"He is coming. Jesus is coming to give repentant sinners His righteousness and His family name. Yes, He is coming, but He is also here right now, demonstrating His strong and capable father-nature to me. I am safe and secure in His family."*

God the Father sent His Son to bring us the heart-transforming combination of grace and truth

"And the Word became flesh and dwelt among us, and we have seen his glory, glory as of the only Son from the Father, full of grace and truth."

When Jesus stooped to join humanity here on Earth, He demonstrated through His life and words the grace and truth that set us free. His grace tells us we cannot earn our way toward His acceptance without Him, and His truth shows us how to live a God-honoring life. Jesus' example on Earth is our roadmap to life and holiness.

Do you sometimes feel distance between you and God? You can ask for His forgiveness and seek His grace to help you where you are in need. Do you feel stuck in some area of your life? You need God's truth from the Bible, which sets you free.

PRAYER: *"Lord, I confess I need You in so many ways. When I try to do things on my own, I see again how much I need Your daily grace to bring me back to closeness with You. Where I feel stuck in a sin pattern, I ask You for Your words of truth to guide me."*

DECLARATION: *"He is coming. Jesus is coming with grace and truth—just exactly what I need! Yes, He is coming, but He is also here right now, enabling me to draw near to Him and live for Him every day."*

Make room. Crown Him King. He is here!

"And while they were there, the time came for her to give birth. And she gave birth to her firstborn son and wrapped him in swaddling cloths and laid him in a manger, because there was no place for them in the inn."

Imagine the innkeeper's chagrin when he found out he hadn't made room for the Son of God to be born. Mary and Joseph made the barn and the manger work just fine, but their Son was worthy of so much more. Later, when Jesus taught, some heard Him, and some did not; some made space for Him, and some did not. Today, we make room for God!

When you make space for Jesus, you welcome Him to be the King in your life, the Ruler, the Guide, and the One Who Cares. What a glorious day to celebrate that the King has come!

PRAYER: *"Lord, I have made space for You in my heart and life. I crown You King. You are in charge here. I welcome You today. I make space for You."*

DECLARATION: *"He is here! Today I celebrate the coming of Jesus. He is the One who has turned my life around, from living for myself to living for Him. His love for me is unchanging. His powerful work in me is demonstrating to all around me the greatness of my God. My Jesus is here with me."*

ACKNOWLEDGMENTS

Every work of God is a team effort in order that God would receive the ultimate credit. Thank you to my daughter, Amelia, for using your creative gift to illustrate. I love you! My long-time friend (and matron of honor), Amy Ruff, edited every page of this devotional. She was also part of educating every one of my children. Thanks to Ethan Ramirez for working on every detail to pull together the publishing of this book. You are one amazing young man. Thank you to every person who encouraged me when I wrote my first version of *He Is Coming, He Is Here* (based upon the book of Isaiah).

But mostly, thank you, my dear husband, Kendrick. You picked out scriptures. You believed in me. You encouraged me. You were determined to see this vision become a reality to bless people.